Life in the
THIRTEEN COLONIES

New Jersey

Jon Sterngass and Matthew Kachur

children's press®
An imprint of
SCHOLASTIC

Library of Congress Cataloging-in-Publication Data

Sterngass, Jon.
 New Jersey / by Jon Sterngass and Matthew Kachur.
   p. cm. — (Life in the thirteen colonies)
 Includes bibliographical references and index.
 ISBN 0-516-24574-0
 1. New Jersey—History—Colonial period, ca. 1600–1775—Juvenile literature. 2. New Jersey—History—
1775–1865—Juvenile literature. I. Kachur, Matthew, 1960– II. Title. III. Series.
 F137.S74 2004
 974.9'02—dc22

                              2004008872

1 2 3 4 5 6 7 8 9 10 R 13 12 11 10 09 08 07 06 05 04

A Creative Media Applications Production
Design: Fabia Wargin Design
Production: Alan Barnett, Inc.
Editor: Matt Levine
Copy Editor: Laurie Lieb
Proofreader: Tania Bissell
Content Research: Lauren Thogersen
Photo Researcher: Annette Cyr
Content Consultant: David Silverman, Ph.D.

Photo Credits © 2004: Bridgeman Art Library International Ltd., London/New York: 53 (John Judkyn Memorial, Bath,
Avon, UK); Colonial Williamsburg Foundation: 61 top left; Corbis Images: cover top right, 84, 88, 93, 97 (Bettmann), 57
(Dave G. Houser), 61 center (James Marshall), 49 (David Muench), 37 (Carl & Ann Purcell), 61 bottom right (Joel W.
Rogers), 60 top right (Royalty-Free), 109 (Joseph Sohm/ChomoSohm Inc.), 101, 119 top right (Joseph Sohm/Visions of
America), 60 left, 61 top right (Nik Wheeler), 6, 31, 110, 118 top; Corbis Sygma/Della Zuana Pascal: 60 bottom right, 61
bottom left; Hulton|Archive/Getty Images: cover center background, cover bottom left, 50, 68, 118-119 background; North
Wind Picture Archives: 54 (Nancy Carter), cover top left, cover bottom right, title page, 2, 10, 12, 16, 21, 22, 24, 27, 29, 32,
39, 41, 45, 46, 62, 66, 71, 74, 76, 80, 91, 104, 107, 113, 118 bottom left, 118 bottom right, 119 top left, 119 bottom; The
Historical Society of Pennsylvania, Philadelphia, PA: 86 (Shippen Portrait Collection, #217).

CONTENTS

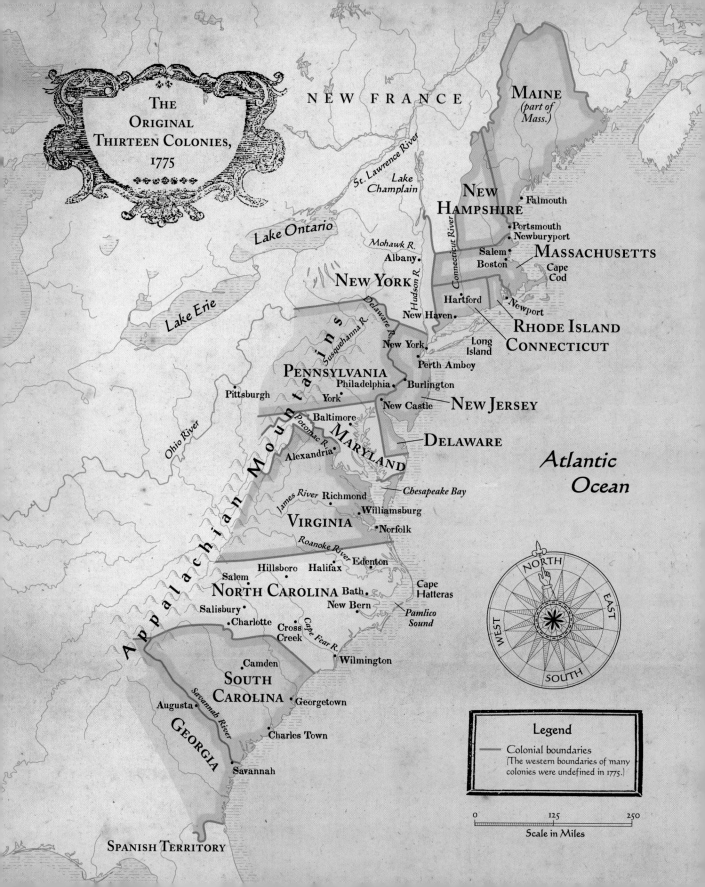

THE ORIGINAL THIRTEEN COLONIES, 1775

NEW FRANCE

MAINE
(part of Mass.)

St. Lawrence River

Lake Champlain

Lake Ontario

Lake Erie

Mohawk R.

Albany

NEW HAMPSHIRE

• Falmouth

• Portsmouth
• Newburyport

Salem •
Boston •

MASSACHUSETTS

Cape Cod

NEW YORK

Hudson R.

Connecticut River

Hartford •

New Haven •

Newport •

RHODE ISLAND
CONNECTICUT

Delaware R.

Susquehanna R.

New York •

Long Island

Perth Amboy •

PENNSYLVANIA

Philadelphia •

• Burlington

Pittsburgh •

York •

New Castle •

NEW JERSEY

Baltimore •

Potomac R.

MARYLAND

DELAWARE

Ohio River

Alexandria •

James River

Richmond •

Chesapeake Bay

• Williamsburg

VIRGINIA

• Norfolk

Atlantic Ocean

Roanoke River

Hillsboro •

Halifax •

Edenton •

Salem •

NORTH CAROLINA

Bath •

Cape Hatteras

Salisbury •

New Bern •

Pamlico Sound

• Charlotte

Cross Creek •

Cape Fear R.

Camden •

Wilmington •

SOUTH CAROLINA

• Georgetown

Augusta •

Savannah River

GEORGIA

• Charles Town

Savannah •

Appalachian Mountains

SPANISH TERRITORY

NORTH
EAST
WEST
SOUTH

Legend

——— Colonial boundaries
(The western boundaries of many colonies were undefined in 1775.)

0   125   250
Scale in Miles

A Nation Grows
From Thirteen Colonies

New Jersey lies in the northeastern region of the United States. The Atlantic Ocean forms its eastern border. Pennsylvania lies to the west, Delaware to the south, and New York to the north. New Jersey was one of the original thirteen colonies.

The Lenni-Lenape Indians lived on the land that would one day become New Jersey for thousands of years before it was settled by European colonists. Little by little, they were forced from the land as the colony's rich soil attracted farmers and manufacturers. African slaves became an important part of New Jersey's colonial history as the farmers needed more workers to harvest the crops.

When the time came for revolution, New Jersey was the location of more battles than any other colony. It would become the third state to ratify the U.S. Constitution.

The map shows the thirteen English colonies in 1775. The colored sections show the areas that were settled at that time.

CHAPTER ONE

Europeans Invade North America

Native American Life

Long before Europeans ever set foot on the land that would become New Jersey, the area was inhabited by Native Americans. The Lenni-Lenape tribe lived around the Delaware River. This area included present-day New Jersey, Delaware, eastern Pennsylvania, and southeastern New York.

The New Jersey Lenni-Lenape lived in a beautiful land of ocean beaches, river valleys, deep forests, and rocky highlands. They lived in harmony with the land, taking from nature only what they needed to survive. They farmed, they fished, and they hunted. They built their homes from the trees and grasses that grew nearby.

The Lenni-Lenape Indians of New Jersey lived in the region between the Delaware River and the Atlantic Ocean.

The Lenni-Lenape lived in villages made up of either round wigwams or longhouses. Wigwams were created with tree branches that were driven into the ground and curved to form a frame. The frame was then covered with tree bark, animal skins, and grass mats. A hole in the top of the wigwam allowed smoke from the cooking fire to escape. Some Lenni-Lenape lived in larger structures called longhouses because more family members could fit inside.

Lenni-Lenape villages were made up of many of these wigwams and longhouses. Between 50 and 200 people typically lived in a village. Each village usually also had a separate house for meetings.

Lenni-Lenape Family

Families were very important to the Lenni-Lenape. They identified themselves by their membership in **clans**, which are groups of related families. Every person belonged to the same clan as his or her mother. Women held almost all Lenni-Lenape property and owned all clan lands.

When a woman and a man got married, the husband would move into a longhouse or wigwam with his wife's family. A wedding joined together not only a man and a woman, but also their families. Because of this custom, women from the same clan stayed together across many generations.

Women played an important role in Lenni-Lenape survival. While men hunted and traded, women gathered wild food and tended gardens. They also made baskets, cooked food, and cared for their children.

From one season to the next, the Lenni-Lenape traveled to make the best use of their land. In the late spring, they planted corn, beans, and squash around villages. In the summer, they traveled to the seashore to fish and gather oysters and clams. In the fall, the Lenni-Lenape moved back to their villages to harvest their crops and dry the food to preserve it for the cold months ahead. In the winter, most Lenni-Lenape stayed in their longhouses or wigwams. They sat around cooking fires where they told stories, sang songs, and danced in thanksgiving.

The Three Sisters

The Lenni-Lenape were excellent farmers. Their villages were surrounded by gardens and fields of crops. Their three major crops were corn, beans, and squash, which made up a large portion of their diet. The Indians called these crops the Three Sisters. They planted the Three Sisters together in mounds. This helped all three plants grow. The beans supplied nitrogen, a rich fertilizer, to the soil. This made the other two plants grow stronger. The beanstalks grew up around the corn, using the cornstalks for support. Finally, the squash leaves shaded the mound and helped keep the soil moist.

European Explorers

In 1524, anywhere from 5,000 to 25,000 Lenni-Lenape were living in the New Jersey region. That year, a ship appeared off the coast of an area called Sandy Hook. The ship's captain was an Italian explorer named Giovanni da Verrazano. He had been hired by the French to search for a shortcut from Europe to Asia. Verrazano was the first

Lenni-Lenape watched from the shore as the first European ships sailed into what would one day be New York Harbor.

European the Native Americans had ever seen. It would be 85 years before another European would visit the land of the Lenni-Lenape.

In 1609, an English explorer named Henry Hudson was exploring the eastern coast of North America. He had been hired by a Dutch company to look for the shortcut that Verrazano had never found. European traders and explorers would travel to Asia seeking the exotic spices and silk that were in demand throughout Europe. To reach Asia, ships had to sail south from Europe all the way around the tip of Africa and head east. The trip was dangerous. The round-trip journey also took more than a year. If a shorter, safer water route from Europe to the Far East could be found, it would mean easier, quicker trips and greater wealth.

The Dutch Press Their Claim

Hudson reported that he "found a river [the Kill van Kull] to the westward, between two islands, the lands…were as pleasant with grass and flowers, and goodly trees, as ever they had seen, and very sweet smells came from them." Hudson and his crew had passed by New Jersey.

Based on Hudson's visit, the Dutch claimed most of the land that is now New Jersey, New York, Delaware, and Connecticut. They called this area New Netherland, after their home, the Netherlands (also called Holland) in Europe.

The Dutch continued to explore North America. Between 1614 and 1624, Cornelius Mey, another Dutch explorer, made several voyages up the Delaware River. (Cape May was later named for him.)

In 1621, the Dutch government allowed a group of merchants to organize the Dutch West India Company. The company started a colony right in the heart of Lenni-Lenape homeland. The Dutch built a small outpost named Fort Nassau in the 1620s. The settlement was on the Delaware River, on the present-day site of Gloucester.

Dutch Settlers

The Dutch West India Company traded brass and iron kettles, guns, blankets, and rum to the Lenni-Lenape in exchange for animal skins and furs. To encourage Dutch farmers to settle in New Netherland, the Dutch West India Company began the **patroon** system in 1629. A Dutch settler could get a huge piece of land along a river in New Netherland by agreeing to establish a settlement of at least fifty people within four years. One patroonship that was successful was Pavonia, which became Jersey City.

Unfortunately for the Dutch, the patroon system failed to attract enough farmers. As a result, the Dutch West India

Company allowed colonists to become fur traders. The possibility of making a fortune in beaver pelts immediately encouraged settlers to spread throughout the area. Trading posts were set up around the New Jersey area. But by then, the Dutch had competition in settling the lands around the Hudson and Delaware rivers. The European country of Sweden had begun exploring the New World.

New Sweden

The New Sweden Company created settlements on the Delaware River in parts of what are now Pennsylvania, Delaware, and New Jersey. According to one seventeenth-century account,

> some Swedish soldiers, who had been in the service of the West India Company in North America, went to Sweden, and there made known the fact that the country was so large that the Hollanders [Dutch] could not possess it all... and that it was only necessary to go there with a small number of people to take possession of it, as no one in that country was powerful enough to prevent it.

This map shows the colony of New Sweden and a picture of Queen Christina (the "Girl King") of Sweden who reigned over the colony.

In 1638, the first Swedish men and women reached the Delaware River. Over the next seventeen years, eight more Swedish expeditions landed in New Sweden.

Johan Printz served as governor of New Sweden from 1643 to 1653. He was a former lieutenant colonel in the

Swedish army and weighed more than 400 pounds (180 kilograms). The Lenni-Lenape called him "big belly."

Printz was a strict governor. He worked hard to help New Sweden grow. He assigned land to farmers. He established trade relations with the natives and other Europeans in the area. He built forts so New Sweden would be protected. Unfortunately, there weren't enough soldiers to occupy the forts. Fort Elfsborg, the largest of the forts, had only 13 soliders. It was also located in a swampy area filled with mosquitos.

In 1653, a Swedish mapmaker described the land on the east bank of the Delaware River as "entirely fertile and suitable for tobacco plantations, and beautiful and rare fruit trees, with fine pasture land and many beautiful valleys, and fine streams which ran up into the country." However, like their Dutch rivals, the Swedes had trouble attracting farmers. The colony never numbered more than 400 people. A **census** in 1644 listed only 121 male adults. No colonists came to New Sweden at all between 1647 and 1654.

The Dutch Conquer New Sweden

Although New Sweden was not very large, it threatened Dutch control over the fur trade in the Delaware Valley. In 1651, Peter Stuyvesant, the governor of New Netherland, attacked New Sweden unsuccessfully. He returned in 1655

Log Cabins

In New Sweden, farmers built traditional Swedish rectangular houses made of logs. The logs were notched together at the corners. The cracks between the logs were filled with a mixture of wood chips, moss, and clay. These New Jersey farmers were probably the first people in North America to build this type of log cabin.

The log cabin was one of the simplest, cheapest, and most quickly built forms of housing for a farmer. A settler could build one of these houses with only an ax and no other hardware. The log cabin became popular with poorer colonists and spread far and wide across America.

Log cabins were easy to build and made good use of local materials.

The Nothnagle House, a log cabin in Gibbstown, New Jersey, was built in 1638. It is often called the oldest standing wooden structure in North America.

with seven armed ships and as many soldiers as the entire population of New Sweden. The Swedes surrendered without firing a shot and Stuyvesant placed New Sweden under Dutch control.

The Pig War

Before Peter Stuyvesant became governor of New Netherland, the colony was governed by Willem Kieft. From 1639 to 1643, Kieft made a series of decisions that would change the course of New Jersey history.

The first thing that Kieft did was to tax the Indian tribes in the area. However, the Indians saw no reason to pay taxes. The Dutch had come to the region uninvited. They also had never repaid all the food the natives had given them and they had not protected the natives in any way. The Indians refused to follow Kieft's laws.

Kieft was furious, but he did nothing. Then in 1641, he found his opportunity to take action. A Dutch farmer accused a group of Indians of stealing his pigs when the animals wandered onto Indian lands. Kieft sent eighty soliders to punish the Indians and force them to pay taxes. At least four Indians and four Dutch settlers were killed. The Pig War had begun.

The peaceful relationship between the Dutch and the Indians was gone. For two years there were small clashes, but no big fights. Then one day, an Indian killed a Dutchman. As a child, this Indian had seen his uncle murdered by some Dutch workmen. He waited until he was older to take revenge, as was the custom of his tribe. When he couldn't find the actual murderers, he killed another Dutchman instead. The Indians thought this was just and fair.

Governor Kieft didn't care about the Indians' sense of justice. He saw his chance to take action and quickly grabbed it. He ordered his soldiers to cross the Hudson and massacre the Indians on the New Jersey side. More than eighty Lenni-Lenape men, women, and children were slaughtered, many in their sleep.

More than 200 settlers and 1,000 Indians died in the war that followed, known as Kieft's War. Native Americans almost wiped out all European settlements west of the Hudson River.

The First Town

Because of the fighting, the New Netherland government would only allow settlers to settle villages on the New Jersey side of the Hudson. This side of the river could be more easily defended. In 1660, they chose to build a town around a trading post that had been there since around 1620. They named it Bergen.

Bergen was the first real European town in New Jersey. As more colonists settled in Bergen, the town grew rapidly. By 1662, Bergen had its own local government, court, and sheriff. Many New Jersey towns would model themselves after Bergen in the years that followed.

Dutch Slavery

Willem Kieft was more than just the cause of fighting between native tribes and the new colonists. He also helped to bring slavery to New Netherland.

The first African residents of New Jersey were slaves who were probably captured by pirates in the early 1600s. They were sold in New Netherland to work on a plantation in Pavonia, along the Delaware River. Because Holland did not recognize slavery at home, the status of these Africans was at first unclear. There were no laws yet in North America to make slavery legal.

After 1640, Dutch settlers demanded more slaves to solve the labor shortage on their farms. In 1644, Governor Kieft observed, "Negroes would accomplish more work for their masters and at less expense, than [Dutch] farm servants, who must be bribed to go thither by a great deal of money and promises." Although Dutch slavery was less brutal than the later English variety, it still meant that human beings were considered property to be bought and sold at the whim of an owner.

By 1660, New Amsterdam (present-day New York City) was the most important slave port in North America. This colony had the largest population of slaves. Some slaves labored on large plantations in present-day New Jersey, such as Nicholas Verlieth's farm in Bergen. By the end of Dutch rule, slavery was well established in New Netherland. The colony's African population was about 800, or 10 percent of the total population.

Slaves lived in crude cabins called "slave quarters" on large farms and plantations.

The English Replace the Dutch

In the early 1660's England's King Charles II looked at a map of America and decided it was time for New Netherland to come under English rule. So, in 1663, King Charles II gave his younger brother James, the Duke of York, all of the land claimed by the Dutch between what are now the states of Maine and Maryland. Of course, the Dutch occupied all this land. All James had to do was take the territory away from the Dutch.

James was the commander of the English Navy. In 1664, James sent four warships and 400 soldiers to New Netherland. Once Peter Stuyvesant saw the guns aimed at New Amsterdam, he surrendered. The rest of the Dutch territories quickly fell into English hands.

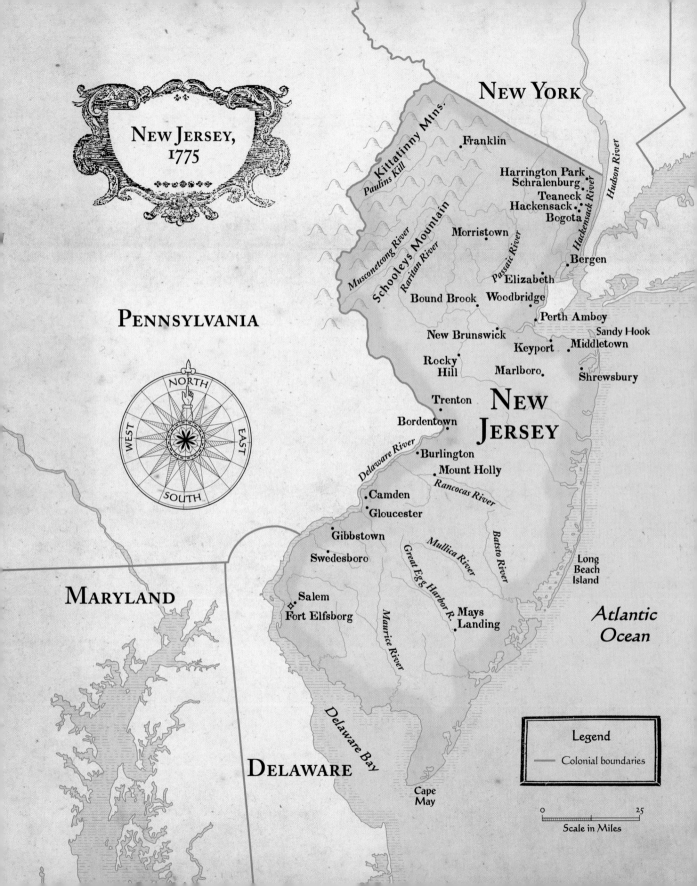

NEW JERSEY, 1775

NEW YORK

PENNSYLVANIA

NEW JERSEY

MARYLAND

DELAWARE

Atlantic Ocean

Kittatinny Mtns.
Paulins Kill
Musconetcong River
Schooley's Mountain
Raritan River
Passaic River
Hackensack River
Hudson River
Delaware River
Rancocas River
Mullica River
Batsto River
Great Egg Harbor R.
Maurice River
Delaware Bay

Franklin
Harrington Park
Schralenburg
Teaneck
Hackensack
Bogota
Bergen
Morristown
Elizabeth
Woodbridge
Bound Brook
Perth Amboy
Sandy Hook
New Brunswick
Keyport
Middletown
Rocky Hill
Marlboro
Shrewsbury
Trenton
Bordentown
Burlington
Mount Holly
Camden
Gloucester
Gibbstown
Swedesboro
Long Beach Island
Salem
Fort Elfsborg
Mays Landing
Cape May

NORTH
WEST
EAST
SOUTH

Legend
—— Colonial boundaries

0   25
Scale in Miles

CHAPTER TWO

An English Colony

New Jersey as a Colony

When the English conquered New Netherland in 1664, the area now known as New Jersey had very few settlers. Some Europeans had settled on the east bank of the Delaware River. Some Dutch men and women lived on the west shore of the Hudson. There was a four-year-old village at Bergen. The rest of the territory remained unbroken wilderness almost unknown to Europeans.

By the time King Charles II came to the throne in 1660, England owned thriving colonies in Massachusetts and Virginia. Charles was extremely generous. He rewarded wealthy men who supported him by giving them 3 million acres in America. During his reign, six colonies were founded or came under English rule in North America: New Jersey, New York, Pennsylvania, North Carolina, South Carolina, and Delaware. These were all proprietary colonies.

This map shows how New Jersey looked in 1775.

Proprietors were people who were given large blocks of land by the king. They hoped to make money by selling or renting this land.

George Carteret

George Carteret was an expert sailor who had fought loyally for King Charles II. During the English Civil War, he had allowed Charles II to stay at his home on the Island of Jersey in the English Channel. In 1664, King James rewarded Carteret and John Berkeley, a British nobleman, by giving them enormous land grants south and southwest of the Hudson Valley. Because of Carteret's connection to the Isle of Jersey, the new lands were known as New Jersey.

New Jersey was under the proprietorship of Berkeley and Carteret from 1664 to 1674. But neither man had the slightest intention of actually taking charge of the colony. Instead, George Carteret appointed Philip Carteret, his distant cousin, as the first colonial governor of New Jersey.

In many other British colonies, European settlers could not freely practice their religion. Berkeley and Carteret tried to attract settlers to New Jersey with the promise of religious freedom, as well as generous land grants. In 1665, in a document called Concessions and Agreement, the proprietors promised that each community in New Jersey could choose its own type of religious worship.

British royal governor Philip Carteret landed in New Jersey in 1665.

Communities were not allowed to deny other people the right to choose their own preachers or ministers.

This tolerant policy soon drew religious groups such as Presbyterians, Quakers, Puritans, and Anglicans to New Jersey. Each group founded small settlements, with village greens and a central square. The landscape of New Jersey became dotted with these small towns. Farmers flocked to the valleys of Hackensack, Passaic, and the Raritan rivers.

The Lenni-Lenape
Lose Their Homeland

There were no major struggles between Europeans and the Lenni-Lenape in New Jersey after 1655. But the Europeans had unknowingly brought something deadly to the New World—disease. Smallpox and measles killed thousands of Lenni-Lenape. In every colony, far more Indians died from these diseases than from the guns of Europeans. The Lenni-Lenape, weakened by disease, alcoholism, and warfare, began to sell their land and move to Pennsylvania and Ohio.

The Lenni-Lenape were forced to leave their homes in New Jersey and move west into Pennsylvania and Ohio.

In addition, the Lenni-Lenape and the Europeans viewed land differently. The Lenni-Lenape traditionally viewed land as a gift from the Creator to be shared and held in common by all members of the tribe. But European colonists thought of land as private property that could be owned, bought, and sold. At first, this difference led to a great deal of misunderstanding and conflict between the Lenni-Lenape and the settlers.

By the late 1600s, however, most Lenni-Lenape were willing to bargain for the sale of their land. Between 1630 and 1767, Lenni-Lenape leaders, often women, put their marks on nearly 800 land sale deeds. Between 1675 and 1716, Weequehala, known as "the Indian King of East New Jersey," signed more than twenty deeds giving up Lenni-Lenape land in Monmouth and Middlesex counties. Almost all Lenni-Lenape land was in European hands by the mid-1700s.

New Jersey Divides in Two

In 1674, John Berkeley lost interest in New Jersey and sold his share of the colony to two English Quakers, John Fenwick and Edward Byllynge. The Quakers, also known as the Society of Friends, were persecuted in Europe for their religious beliefs. They thought they could practice their religion in peace if they left England and organized their own colonies in America.

First Quaker meetinghouse in Burlington was built in 1683 in the shape of a hexagon.

In 1676, Byllynge went bankrupt. Meanwhile, he and Fenwick were disagreeing about many issues. Quaker leader William Penn and a group of men stepped in and took control of West Jersey while Carteret kept his interest in East Jersey. This agreement is sometimes known as the Quintipartite Deed of 1676. It divided New Jersey into two parts, giving the Quakers the eastern bank of the Delaware River. The two Jersey colonies would not be reunited until 1702.

The first Quaker settlements in West Jersey were Salem, established in 1675, and Burlington, founded in 1677. As the persecution of English Quakers increased at the end of King Charles II's reign, Quakers began to flee England in greater numbers. Almost 2,000 Quakers moved to West Jersey in 1682 alone.

Concessions and Agreements of 1677

The Quakers wanted to attract settlers who wished to practice their religion without persecution. The leaders of the colony issued a document known as the West New Jersey Concessions and Agreements of 1677. This established the government and laws for the people settling in the colony. The is one of the first American documents to guarantee individual freedoms.

The concessions gave all lawmaking powers to an assembly chosen by the "inhabitants, freeholders and proprietors" of the colony. Local officeholders would also be elected. Complete freedom of religion and a guarantee of trial by jury were included. Imprisonment for debt was not permitted. The assembly was not allowed to take away any rights given in the concessions.

New Jersey Becomes a Royal Colony

When Queen Anne came to the English throne in 1702, she demanded that the proprietors give their rights of government back to England. By now, the proprietors of East and West Jersey were fed up with the problems of running their colonies. They gladly returned their governmental powers to the English crown. They kept the land they had been given.

The British government united East and West Jersey into a single colony in 1702. Although New Jersey's independence from New York was also recognized that year, New Jersey's first governor, Edward Hyde, Lord Cornbury, was already the governor of New York. The governor of New York would also run New Jersey until 1738.

A Growing Colony

By the mid-1700s, it was clear that the colony of New Jersey was thriving. From about 10,000 residents in 1703, New Jersey had grown to 61,000 in 1745. The colony contained people of many different nationalities, including the Dutch, Swedish, English, Scots, and Africans.

But all groups were not treated equally. The majority of Africans living in New Jersey were enslaved. In 1737 one out of every five Bergen County residents and one out of every six Somerset County residents were slaves. A census in 1745 listed more than 800 enslaved blacks in Middlesex and Monmouth counties. In that same year, one out of every fourteen New Jersey residents was a slave.

Ships such as the Grev Bernstorf *brought slaves from Africa to New Jersey and the other American colonies. Between 1740 and 1757, at least 290 slaves came to the shores of America through the New Jersey port of Perth Amboy.*

Slavery on New Jersey Farms

Slave labor was very important on colonial New Jersey farms. In eastern New Jersey, the slave population of about 100 in 1680 rose to almost 2,000 in fifty years. Slaves made up about 40 percent of the labor supply in Bergen County and more than 30 percent in nearby Somerset County. No county in eastern New Jersey had more single white men than slaves on the tax lists of 1751 and 1769.

Advertisements for slaves to be sold in New Jersey described more than three-quarters of them as farmers. On New Jersey's farms, slaves often worked next to free whites. They helped in raising wheat, corn, and rye, tending orchards and meadows, herding and feeding animals, and cutting firewood.

A farm owner rarely had more than three slaves, so it was almost impossible for black families to live together. Children old enough to work were often separated from their mother and father. Slaves could not move anywhere unless they were sold. They could not own land or choose their masters. When white farmers died, they often wrote wills that gave their slaves away to other people. It was hard for slaves to have any sense of hope for their future.

The colony did have a small free black community. Three of the original landholders of Tappan were free black farmers. Youngham Roberts, a freeborn black, purchased 200 acres (80 hectares) and became one of the first residents of Hackensack.

Slave quarters had few comforts and slave children worked instead of attending school.

However, in 1714, the New Jersey Assembly passed a law requiring slave owners to pay 200 pounds before freeing a slave. (This was equal to about $35,000 today.) Most slave owners would not do this, so very few slaves were freed in colonial New Jersey. This greatly limited the number of free black farmers. Over the next 50 years, the New Jersey legislature would pass many laws that took away the rights of slaves. While the rest of the colonists in New Jersey thrived, it would be many, many years before slaves would see any freedoms at all.

Slave Laws

In 1714, the Freedom of Movement law was passed. Any black found traveling without a license, or not on his master's business, was to be whipped and to remain in prison until the costs of his capture had been paid by his owner.

In 1751, the Freedom of Assembly law was passed. It forbid large meetings of blacks. It also required slaves to be home by 9 P.M. This law also stated that slaves could go to church, funeral services, and run errands with permission from their master.

Negroes for Sale.

A Cargo of very fine stout Men and Women, in good order and fit for immediate service, just imported from the Windward Coast of Africa, in the Ship Two Brothers.——

Conditions are one half Cash or Produce, the other half payable the first of January next, giving Bond and Security if required.

The Sale to be opened at 10 o'Clock each Day, in Mr. Bourdeaux's Yard, at No. 48, on the Bay.

May 19, 1784.   JOHN MITCHELL.

Thirty Seafoned Negroes

To be Sold for Credit, at Private Sale.

AMONGST which is a Carpenter, none of whom are known to be dishonest.

Also, to be fold for Cash, a regular bred young Negroe Man-Cook, born in this Country, who ferved feveral Years under an exceeding good French Cook abroad, and his Wife a middle aged Wafher-Woman, (both very honeft) and their two Children. *Likewife.* a young Man a Carpenter.

For Terms apply to the Printer.

Newspaper advertisements announcing slaves for sale were common throughout New Jersey and the other colonies.

CHAPTER THREE
The Garden Colony

A Fertile Land

New Jersey's reputation as "the garden state" goes back to the colonial period. Unlike Europe, New Jersey had thousands of acres of rich soil that had not been worn out from centuries of hard use. The long growing season attracted settlers who dreaded the cold winters and rocky soil of Massachusetts. In the New England colonies, a family of five needed a farm of about 125 acres (50 hectares) to live in comfort. In New Jersey, a family needed only about 90 acres (36 hectares). New Jersey farmers often raised twice as much wheat per acre as farmers in the New England colonies.

Early settlers generously praised New Jersey's land. One farmer wrote: "The country is so good that I do not see how it can reasonably be found fault with."

In colonial times, oxen were used to pull heavy carts on New Jersey farms.

A Colony of Small Farms

In the 1600s, many farms in New Jersey were larger than 500 acres (200 hectares), but the average size had dropped to 200 acres (80 hectares) by the 1740s. Some New Jersey farms were so small that they only fed the family members who owned and worked on the land.

Many communities were **self-sufficient**. The people made almost everything they needed and traded with each other for the things they couldn't make themselves. The settlers cut down forests, cleared the land, and built houses. Like the Lenni-Lenape, they grew corn and beans. They also grew wheat and oats and used the grains to make bread. New Jersey farmers also used some land for grazing animals and growing hay.

Some farms became large enough to sell their extra harvests. Eastern New Jersey supplied the markets of New York with grains, fruits, and vegetables. Western New Jersey played the same role for Philadelphia.

Growing Wheat

The population of Europe grew quickly in the 1700s, and there was tremendous demand for American grains. Wheat prices doubled between 1720 and 1770. By 1775, wheat, corn, flour, and bread shipped from the middle colonies

Farm Animals

Unlike farms today, colonial New Jersey farms had no tractors. They depended on animals to do the hard work. Oxen were often used, because they were stronger and calmer than horses. Horses were used mainly for transportation. Even small farms raised cows, chickens, pigs, and sheep. Local New Jersey laws did not put limits on where farm animals could roam. If people objected, they could build fences to keep the animals off their property.

made up more than 15 percent of the value of all American exports. A great deal of New Jersey's wheat also went to the sugar colonies of the Caribbean.

In the 1740s, New Jersey actually produced more wheat than New York or Pennsylvania. One colonial observer claimed that "the first crop of wheat will fully pay [a farmer] for all the expense he has been at, in clearing up, sowing, and fencing his land; and at the same time increases the value of land, eight or ten times the original cost." Hunterdon County produced more wheat than any other county in the colonies. This county was sometimes called New Jersey's breadbasket.

Despite this, it was difficult for a farmer to grow wheat in large quantities in the 1700s. Workers used hand **sickles** to cut the grain. A worker with a sickle could harvest only about half an acre of wheat a day. This was a problem because wheat has to be cut at exactly the right time, or the dry grain falls to the ground and is lost.

In the 1750s, the cradle scythe was invented. This was a long-handled tool with a sharp blade and wooden fingers that cradled the cut grain. The cradle made it easier to collect the grain. Even with cradles, however, a family with two adults could not usually harvest more than 200 bushels (7,000 liters) of grain in a season. Any wheat not needed by the family could be sold. With this money, the family members might buy goods such as salt, sugar, tools, and cloth. They also might try to buy a few more acres of land.

Mill and the Miller

In order to make flour for bread, grain had to be ground. Almost every colonial village began with a miller who ground the local farmers' grain. A mill required a stream with enough force to turn a waterwheel. The waterwheel powered the mill. Weavers, carpenters, tanners, and shoemakers often settled next to mills. In this way, small villages were born.

Waterpower operated many types of colonial equipment. One of the earliest sawmills in New Jersey was established in Woodbridge in 1682. Mills could also grind tobacco or grind clay for pottery. They could even cut iron and operate spinning gears used in simple machinery.

Millstones

Grist usually refers to grain that has to be ground. Gristmills used a pair of millstones with grooves in them. These millstones varied in size from 4 to 6 feet (1.2 to 1.8 meters) and weighed as much as 1 ton (0.9 metric tons). The distance between the two stones could be adjusted, depending on whether the miller was grinding corn, rye, or wheat. The stones had to be perfectly balanced and could not touch each other, or they would be ruined.

Water provided the power to turn the wheel used to grind corn, wheat, and other grains in New Jersey mills.

Women in Colonial New Jersey

Colonial New Jersey farms were worked by men, women and children alike. These farms could not have survived without the hard work of women. Farm women, helped by their children, performed hundreds of required household tasks. They produced, preserved, and cooked food. Children churned butter and made candles and soap. Thread was spun from wool and woven into shirts and gowns or knitted into stockings and sweaters. Mothers provided health care and instruction for the family. In addition, women performed

The First Official American Inventor

It is believed that the first official American inventor was a woman. Sybilla Righton Masters was thought to have been born in New Jersey. She invented a machine to prepare Indian corn by stamping it rather than grinding it. This saved time in preparing hominy meal, a common food of colonial New Jersey.

In 1715, Masters received what may have been the first **patent** granted to an American colonist by the British King. The patent was in her husband's name, even though the invention was Sybilla's, because women were not allowed to hold patents. However, Thomas Masters always said that the invention was his wife's idea.

Farm women prepared food and preserved it for the winter. This woman is peeling apples to make dumplings.

the difficult job of raising children. A woman's life was filled with exhausting work.

Almost half of New Jersey's colonial settlers were women. Just as in Europe, New Jersey law and custom gave men more power than women. Once a woman got married, she no longer had the legal right to own any property at all, even land. Everything belonged to her husband.

Women were taught that their role in life was to be a dutiful daughter to a father and a helper to a husband. Divorce was extremely rare.

Most colonial churches did not give women an equal role or allow them to be leaders. The Quakers were an exception. In marriage services, a Quaker woman was never required to promise to "obey" her husband. A French visitor noted that the Quakers believed "that women can be called to the ministry as well as men." Elizabeth Haddon Estaugh, one of the earliest New Jersey Quakers, became a colonial proprietor and founded Haddonfield. She also served as a clerk of Quaker women's meetings in New Jersey for more than fifty years.

Colonial New Jersey women usually married in their twenties and had an average of five to seven children. One couple from Holland moved to Middlebrook in central New Jersey in 1723. They had seventeen children. By the time they both died, the couple had 352 direct descendants.

Children in New Jersey

Most children in colonial New Jersey got very little formal education. They woke as soon as the sun rose in order to help their parents with chores around the farm and house. Only when their chores were done could they go to school.

While many children were taught reading, writing, and arithemetic, this often stopped when the child completed elementary school. More boys than girls were allowed to

The main street of Swedesboro was typical of many prosperous New Jersey towns.

continue their schooling. In addition, only boys were permitted to study subjects such as Latin.

Teachers in colonial times were often strict. If a child was not paying attention in school, the teacher would rap them on the knuckles with a hard object or put them in a corner with a dunce hat on their head. Teachers were even permitted to spank children.

Children in colonial times did not have paper and pencils. They used hornbooks. This was a wooden paddle with a paper with numbers, alphabet letters, or a prayer written on it. The paper was covered with a thin layer of cows horn to protect it.

Widow of Opportunity

In colonial New Jersey, women worked around society's attempts to limit them. In 1700, Blandina Kiersted Bayard bought a large piece of land from the Lenni-Lenape. It made up present-day Mahwah, Oakland, and Franklin Lakes in Bergen County. Bayard was a widow (and mother of five children), so under English law she could control her own property. Fifteen Lenni-Lenape men and four Lenni-Lenape women participated in the sale. In return for the land, they received "divers good causes and several kindnesses," as well as "goods and wares" worth about 120 pounds. (British money that would be equal to about $20,000 today.)

Rural Prosperity

Over time, New Jersey came to be known as a colony with prosperous farms that surrounded small, thriving market towns. Travelers in rural areas of New Jersey often commented on the absence of great estates. They noted that New Jersey's small farmers seemed to live a comfortable life.

In 1744, Dr. Alexander Hamilton took a round-trip journey from Maryland to New Hampshire. He kept a diary while he traveled. Here is the entry for Thursday, June 14:

A little after 5 in the morning, I departed Trenton and rid twelve miles of a very pleasant road well stored with houses of entertainment. The country round displays variety of agreeable prospects and rural scenes. I observed many large fields of wheat, barley, and hemp, which is a great staple and commodity now in this province [New Jersey], but very little maize or Indian corn....All round you in this part of the country you observe a great many pleasant fertile meadows and pastures which diffuse at this season of the year in the cool of the morning, a sweet and refreshing smell.

Transportation and Taverns

One of the reasons people were able to travel to New Jersey and enjoy all that the colony had to offer was the roads. In order for farmers to make a living, they needed to sell what they grew at markets around the colony. So the people of New Jersey built a network of roads to accommodate the growers.

By 1765, New Jersey had more roads than any other colony. The earliest European settlers traveled on trails that had been used by the Lenni-Lenape for centuries. Many of New Jersey's modern roads and highways simply follow these old trails.

The **Jersey wagon**, developed in New Jersey in the 1730s, is sometimes considered the first vehicle invented in colonial America. This huge freight wagon was often covered with cloth. A team of four or six horses was needed to pull it. Only the most daring or poorest people traveled in Jersey wagons, because they had no springs at all and gave very bumpy rides. Jersey wagons usually carried farm products to the markets of Trenton, New Jersey, and Philadelphia.

Ferries were also important to connect New Jersey to Philadelphia and New York City. As early as the 1700s, ferries carried goods and agricultural products back and forth across the Hudson and Delaware rivers.

Wherever there were roads and ferries, there were taverns and inns. These were the main social and political centers of New Jersey society. Almost all public meetings and celebrations were held in taverns. By 1784, there were 443 taverns in New Jersey. This number was equal to one tavern for every 170 male residents.

Taverns were a popular place to gather and enjoy food and drink in colonial New Jersey.

CHAPTER FOUR

Merchants, Miners, and Craftsmen

More Than Just Farmland

In colonial New Jersey, most colonists lived on small farms. However, there was more to the colony than wheat. As the population of New Jersey grew, workers loaded, sailed, and unloaded ships on the Atlantic Ocean and the Delaware River. Miners dug for iron and copper in northern New Jersey. Skilled workers produced fine colonial craftwork, especially in glass, leather, and pottery. New Jersey was already beginning to show the wide range of different jobs and industries that would mark its future as a state.

By 1760, the colony had sixty towns, although many were very small. A town often had nothing more than a church, a courthouse, and an inn. Sometimes there was a

🐟 *Iron works were factories where metal was melted and shaped into useful tools. They were an important part of New Jersey's colonial economy.*

general store, a mill, or a blacksmith's shop. Camden and Jersey City were thriving market towns built around ferry traffic on the Hudson River. Elizabeth, the largest city in New Jersey, had about 1,500 people. New Jersey's farmers could not exist without these small cities and the people who lived there and bought the farmers' products.

Merchants

Before 1700, many merchants lived in New Jersey ports such as Salem, Burlington, and Elizabeth. Perth Amboy, at the mouth of the Raritan River, was the major port.

But New Jersey's ports could not compete with their out-of-state rivals. By the mid-1700s, almost all of New Jersey's wheat, corn, and bread exports shipped out of New York City and Philadelphia. One governor of New Jersey stated, "New York and Philadelphia are in Reality the Commercial Capitals of East and West Jersey; and almost all the Articles we import for Home Consumption are from one or other of those cities." A visitor to Perth Amboy in the 1740s reported, "It is the principal town in New Jersey.... 'Tis a sea port, having a good harbor but small trade."

A merchant's life was risky. In the first few months of 1761 alone, merchants lost what would today be worth millions of dollars of cargo because of shipwrecks. In response, money was raised to build a lighthouse at Sandy

Hook, New Jersey. The eight-sided, 103-foot-high (31-meter) lighthouse first beamed its light over the ocean on the night of June 11, 1764. This lighthouse is the oldest original lighthouse in the United States. It still gleams a New Jersey welcome to passing ships today.

Built in 1764, the eight-sided lighthouse at Sandy Hook still stands today.

Other Seacoast Occupations

New Jersey's rivers and the ocean provided many different types of work. Colonists on the seacoast made a living by fishing and building ships. Boats were built far inland and floated down the rivers to the bay and ocean. New Jersey's seemingly unlimited supply of good lumber supported the fast-growing shipbuilding industry. Many black Americans, both free and enslaved, constructed boats, worked on the docks, and served aboard ships.

Whaling was a dangerous business. Many whalers eventually turned to farming instead.

Although Cape May began as a whaling village in the 1600s, whalers caught only about two whales a year from 1700 to 1760. Turning to farming instead, the whalers bought medium-sized farms and raised cattle, wheat, and corn. By the time of the Revolutionary War, Cape May County was a prosperous community.

Towns around Raritan Bay, north of Sandy Hook, were famous for their oysters in the late 1700s. The village of Keyport was first settled as a large farm in 1714, but it soon became a major oyster center and a port for sending farm goods to New York City. One visitor to the area in the 1740s reported, "They have here the best oysters I have eaten in America."

Pirates in New Jersey

Not all seacoast occupations were legal. Blackbeard was the nickname of a cruel pirate who preyed on ships and coastal settlements of the Caribbean and the Atlantic. According to one legend, Blackbeard sailed up the Delaware River in 1717 and landed in New Jersey on a stormy night. He buried a huge chest full of gold, silver, and jewels beneath a walnut tree in Burlington. One of Blackbeard's sailors and a dog were killed and buried along with the treasure. The pirates believed their ghosts would guard the treasure. Many people claim to have seen the "ghost dog" on Wood Street in Burlington. Another famous pirate, Captain William Kidd, supposedly buried a huge treasure on the beach at Cape May Point in 1699.

The Pottery Industry

New Jersey colonists needed to make the most of their household goods. Although wealthy colonists were able to afford fine china dishes imported from England, most New Jersey colonists used cheaper household goods made in the colony. Pottery made from clay was inexpensive and fireproof and would hold liquids. New Jersey, which had an excellent supply of natural clay, was one of the oldest centers of pottery production in North America. New Jersey potters made plates, bowls, utensils, pitchers, jugs, dishes, and storage jars. The pottery was usually used locally or shipped to New York City and Philadelphia.

About 1686, Daniel Coxe founded a pottery company near Burlington that shipped pottery as far away as Barbados and Jamaica. Coxe also attempted to imitate the thin, white porcelain made by the potters of China, which was known as china. Unfortunately, he noted, there was "noe clay in the Country that would make white ware."

Iron Mining

Northern New Jersey had some of the earliest mines in colonial America. They were established in the Kittatinny Mountains. There were also mines in the other New Jersey

Redware

Most New Jersey potters made redware from plain brick clay that was colored naturally by iron in the soil. Potters would coat redware with a glaze that made it strong and prevented leaks. Most colonial Americans preferred to use gray-blue stoneware that was glazed with salt. Stoneware was the most fashionable material for plates and pots in England. Americans wanted it also. This stoneware had to be imported from England and was very expensive.

branches of the Appalachian Mountains. Workers dug copper and iron ore there.

Lewis Morris is thought to have established New Jersey's earliest ironworks. Morris had become wealthy from the profits of a sugar plantation in Barbados. In 1676, he began the Tinton Falls Iron Works in Shrewsbury, in

Monmouth County. Lewis's 6,000-acre (2,400-hectare) iron forge, mill, and mine were worked by more than sixty slaves.

Other mines, forges, and furnaces quickly opened throughout the colony. In the 1770s, there were more than 100 ironworks in southwestern New York, northern New Jersey, and eastern Pennsylvania. They produced about one-seventh (14 percent) of the world's iron at the time.

Cannonballs were one of New Jersey's main contributions to the American Revolution. They weighed between two and seventy-two pounds each.

Ironworks sometimes developed into small towns with gristmills, sawmills, and shops. Wood from the forests was burned down to charcoal and used as fuel for the furnaces. Water from streams became a power source. New Jersey residents used the iron locally for pots, kettles, and stoves. These products were also transported to other areas up and down the eastern coast of America.

The swamps of southern New Jersey also had important mineral deposits. Iron known as "bog ore" was dug up from the banks of the streams and rivers. The Batsto Iron Works along the Batsto River made both household items and war supplies. It is now a nationally recognized restored colonial village.

Copper and Marl

The Dutch began digging for copper in present-day Warren County in the 1650s. Copper was used for pails, teakettles, funnels, pans, and tubing. If zinc was available from England, copper could be made into brass. Brass is a combination of zinc and copper that makes a much stronger metal.

In 1731, John Schuyler's northeastern New Jersey copper mine exported 1,386 tons (1,247 metric tons) of copper. The copper was mined by more than 200 black slaves. By 1753, Schuyler's copper mine was 200 feet (60 meters) deep. The mine was also filling with water faster than it could be pumped out by hand. Schuyler used one of the first steam engines to pump the water out of the mine.

Another colonial New Jersey natural resource was marl. Marl is a loose, crumbly type of soil consisting mainly of clay and sand. In 1768, colonists discovered that the marl of Monmouth County could be used as fertilizer for certain soils. The village of Marlboro received its name from the new industry.

Tanneries

The colonial tanner made leather from animal skins. New Jersey residents depended on leather for saddles and harnesses for farm animals. Colonists wore clothes made out of leather, such as pants, aprons, caps, shoes, and boots. Tanning leather was a difficult task that took many months.

The Ogden family of Elizabeth began one of New Jersey's first tanneries in 1664. Newark was especially well known for the production of fine leather goods. This was a mixed blessing, because tanning in the colonial era was a very messy business. The smell of lime and decaying animal hides filled the air. No one wanted to live anywhere near a tannery. However, colonists continued to rely on leather for many different products. It was a sturdy material that didn't rip easily and wore well in harsh weather.

Colonial glassmakers used dome-shaped ovens such as this to heat the glass to more than 3,600°F (1,982°C) so it could be shaped and molded.

Glassmaking

Glassmaking in America received its first real start in New Jersey. Caspar Wistar, who came from Germany, began a huge glassworks on a 2,000-acre (800-hectare) site near Salem in 1739. For the next forty years, Wistar's factory produced many different types of glass. It also made hundreds of types of bottles, jars, and pitchers.

Wistar's workers experimented with new procedures. They were the first to fuse together glass of two colors. Wistar's specialty was window glass. This product was rare in the colonies because glass breaks so easily when transported. The Wistarburg Works flourished until 1781.

Several brothers named Stanger studied under Wistar. Then they opened their own glassworks in a separate village in 1779. That town is now called Glassboro. Glassware is still produced there and throughout Salem County.

Early Vacation Spots

New Jersey also proved to be a hot vacation spot for nearby Philadelphians. By the late 1700s, Philadelphia was the busiest seaport and largest city in North America. It had more than 30,000 residents at this time. On hot summer days, the temperature often reached 90 degrees. There were few cooling breezes and no air conditioning. Wealthy Philadelphia residents wanted to get away from the heat, horses, flies, and diseases of the city.

Cape May, on New Jersey's southern tip, was a good place for Philadelphians to go to get away from the city and enjoy the cool breezes of the sea shore. The whaling, farming, and fishing families that lived along New Jersey's coastline began to rent out their houses and build inns along the shore. The area became a retreat for Philadelphia's wealthy merchants. For example, the *Pennsylvania Gazette* ran an advertisement for Cape May land as early as 1766:

TO BE SOLD:

A Valuable Plantation...pleasantly situated,
open to the Sea, in the Lower Precinct of the County of
Cape May, and within One Mile
and a Half of the Sea Shore, where a Number
resort for Health, and bathing in the Water.

Schooley's Mountain was another early New Jersey resort. The beautiful mountain was located about 17 miles (27 kilometers) west of Morristown. A cool mineral water spring there attracted visitors as early as the 1770s. At New Jersey resorts like Cape May and Schooley's Mountain, the American vacation was born.

Today, when people think of a New Jersey resort, they usually think of Atlantic City. However, that resort was not settled until a railroad connected it to Philadelphia in 1852.

Getting around in the colonies took a lot of time
There were no motor powered cars, boats, planes, or
trains. Travel was slow and relied on the muscles of
animals and colonists for power.

☞ *The covered or
Conestoga wagon
was invented in
New Hampshire.
It became the
moving van of the
colonies and was
used to haul large
loads of goods from
place to place.*

☟ *Wealthy colonists rode
in carriages pulled by
horses. Larger carriages
transported people
between towns and cities.*

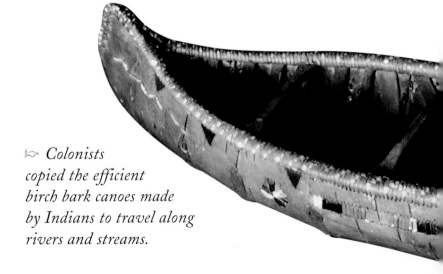

☞ *Colonists
copied the efficient
birch bark canoes made
by Indians to travel along
rivers and streams.*

Around

🪝 Large freight loads were carried up and down rivers by flat-bottomed boats propelled by oars.

☛ *The most common mode of colonial transportation was "shanks mare." Shanks were leg muscles and a mare was a female horse. The expression meant that colonists walked wherever they went.*

🪝 *Most farmers and tradesmen had small wooden carts and wagons to haul everything from family members to farm goods.*

🪝 *Sailing ships brought colonists to America. They also carried colonists and cargo back to Europe and between colonial ports.*

CHAPTER FIVE

Tensions in the Colony

A Colony of Many Different Groups

New Jersey was not like New England or the slave colonies in the South. People of many different languages, religions, and cultures mingled together in the colony. Families moved to New Jersey from New England and Long Island. Immigrants came from the Caribbean, Holland, Belgium, Finland, and France. They also came from Germany, Ireland, Scotland, Sweden, and Wales. People practiced different religions. There were many Puritan, Dutch Reformed, Baptist, Quaker, Lutheran, and Anglican colonists in New Jersey.

Weekly religious services provided New Jersey's colonists a time to meet and socialize as well as practice their religious beliefs.

master, "a pair of iron pothooks around his neck with a chain fastened to it that reached his feet."

Slaves sometimes escaped into New Jersey's swamps and forests in search of freedom.

Stealing goods from a master was one of the few ways slaves could get back at their white owners. A 1682 New Jersey law made it illegal for anyone to purchase goods from slaves. The law stated that "it is found in daily experience, that negro and Indian slaves or servants under the pretense of trade or liberty to traffic, do frequently steal from their masters and others what they expose to sale at a distance from their habitations."

Enslaved Africans sometimes plotted to rise up as a group. In Somerville in 1734, thirty blacks were accused of planning a slave revolt. Another plot may have occurred in Hackensack in 1741. Two slaves were executed by burning for this crime. But even horrible punishments did not stop the slaves' desire for freedom.

Master and Slave

Relations between master and slave in colonial New Jersey could be brutal. In 1739, in Rocky Hill (Somerset County), Robert Hooper's slave was "ordered by the Overseer's wife to bring in some wood and make fire, he replied in a surly tone that he would make fire enough and pursued her with an axe." The slave then killed her son. He also burned the barn, which contained over 1,000 bushels (35,000 liters) of grain. The slave was captured three days later and executed.

Fee Simple

Poor white farmers were much better off than slaves or renters, but they still had their own complaints. They feared that the independent farmers of America were slowly becoming like the poor peasants of Europe.

Most of New Jersey's farms were small and owned by families.

New Jersey farmers wanted to own their land in fee simple. This meant they wanted to own land without any obligations. Instead, sellers of land insisted on charging a **quitrent**. This was a small sum of money that symbolized the authority of the state or lord. Quitrents never ended. Farmers had to pay every year and never felt like they fully owned their land. In addition, to pay a quitrent, a farmer needed "hard" (not paper) money. This was not always easy to find in New Jersey.

When the British took over New Jersey in 1664, the proprietors insisted on the payment of a quitrent. But the New England colonists that the landowners hoped to attract had become used to owning land in fee simple. Many New Jersey proprietors in the 1700s ignored the laws regarding quitrents. But at least some quitrents were collected right up to the time of the Revolutionary War.

The landowners wanted to make money from their land grants. Proprietors always insisted that quitrents were their right, even if they did not collect them. But quitrents set poor farmers against landowners. Whenever sellers and former owners tried to collect quitrents, there was the possibility of violence. Protests against quitrents in 1701 led to mob attacks on local jails. These attacks occurred in Salem, Burlington, and several eastern New Jersey towns.

Rent Riots

Poor New Jersey farmers were often unsure if they even legally owned their land. Some settlers had bought their land from Native Americans. Others bought land from long-gone Dutch and Swedish officials or from competing English landowners. Many new immigrants to New Jersey became "squatters." They refused to even bother getting any title at all but simply settled on open land without any legal claim. Hundreds of squatters occupied land in Hunterdon County. This land was claimed by West Jersey proprietors.

For 100 years after the English conquest, New Jersey's small farmers battled over land titles. In the 1740s and 1750s, violence broke out in eastern New Jersey between squatters and proprietors. The farmers had support from many people in New Jersey. Supporters wrote pamphlets claiming that their "Rights, Properties, and Possessions" had been invaded. Landowners at a meeting in 1746 criticized the rioters for defending titles of land received "from strolling Indians for a few Bottles of Rum."

A Lawful Colony

Just like today, many colonists in the 1700s claimed that Americans liked to use lawyers and courts more than was necessary. In 1744, a visitor to New Jersey noted that "there are so many proprietors that share the lands in New Jersey, and so many doubtful titles and rights that it creates an inexhaustible and profitable pool for the lawyers."

Disorder continued when proprietors tried to evict people by claiming that they did not have lawful title to land. Rioters, squatters, and poor farmers would be arrested. In turn, mobs of angry farmers would attack the jails and release them. Sheriffs and judges were threatened. Armed

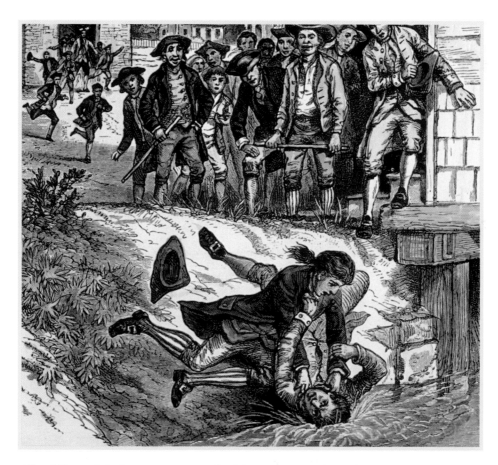

Sheriffs and judges were attacked by angry mobs who came to release farmers whom they thought had been unjustly jailed.

bands of men roamed the countryside, attacking settlers who held land titles from the proprietors.

Between 1745 and 1754, riots took place in rural areas in Hunterdon, Essex, Middlesex, Somerset, Morris, and Bergen counties. There were also riots in Perth Amboy and Newark. Governor Jonathan Belcher asked England for help. However, no instructions or soldiers arrived.

New Jersey farmers were unwilling to accept being poor as a normal condition of life. The colonists were also losing their respect for the royal governor and British rule. Talk of natural rights, freedom, and equality filled the air. What the English did next would set the stage for revolution.

The French and Indian War

From 1754 to 1763, the British and French fought for control of North America. This war was called the French and Indian War. The English finally defeated the French in 1763. By then the British government was in tremendous debt. It had borrowed millions of pounds to fight the war. England decided to tax the American colonies to help pay for the war.

Parliament was the lawmaking body of England. In 1765, Parliament passed a Stamp Act that taxed legal documents, newspapers, and other items. Many colonists were upset because this increased the cost of printed materials. The New Jersey Assembly met in November 1765 and issued a statement that it was "essential to the freedom of a people, and the undoubted right of Englishmen, that no taxes be imposed on them but with their own consent given personally, or by their representatives."

Parliament repealed, or ended, the Stamp Act in 1766. In its place, it passed the Townshend Acts in 1767. The acts taxed imports such as glass, paper, paint, and tea. Once again, there was public complaint in New Jersey and the other colonies. In 1770, Parliament bowed to American pressure. It repealed the Townshend Acts, except for the tax on tea.

After the French and Indian War broke out in 1754, proprietors gradually got back control of the land in New Jersey. They even managed to collect a few quitrents. But for many New Jersey farmers, acting as a group outside of the law was more effective. They noticed that the royal governor had no troops and no control of the local citizen **militia**. Therefore, the governor could not control the disorder. The lack of control, the taxes, and a religious turn of events would influence the course of New Jersey's history.

CHAPTER SIX

The Movement for Independence

~~~~~~

The Great Awakening

A religious movement called the Great Awakening was another factor that influenced colonists to want to break free from England.

The Great Awakening began in the 1720s and quickly swept across America. Preachers roamed the countryside claiming that a personal relationship with God was important. They also said that good behavior and emotional church services were more important than book learning and Bible reading.

New Jersey preachers played a key role in the Great Awakening. Theodore Frelinghuysen was a preacher. He arrived in New Jersey in 1720. As a pastor in Raritan,

During the Great Awakening, churches throughout the colonies were filled with people seeking religious enlightenment.

Frelinghuysen delivered strong sermons. He encouraged members of his congregation to preach. He influenced Presbyterian ministers William Tennent and his son Gilbert. The Tennents helped spread the Great Awakening through New Jersey and Pennsylvania in the 1730s and 1740s.

Country preachers rode from town to town spreading their religious messages.

The Great Awakening encouraged democracy in religion. The beliefs spread by the Great Awakening challenged many established, respected ministers. The Anglican Church was the official church of England. The British government and British leaders in America supported it. New Jersey, however, was a land of many different religious beliefs. The Great Awakening made many New Jersey residents, especially Presbyterians, disapprove of the Anglican Church. People who disliked the Anglican Church were easily persuaded to dislike English rule in general. It was yet another reason for many colonists to want to create an independent nation.

Princeton and Rutgers

Partly as a result of The Great Awakening, New Jersey's first college was founded in 1746. Presbyterians wanted to start a school that would provide a good education for future ministers. So they started the College of New Jersey, now Princeton University.

Queens College, now Rutgers University, was started in 1766 by leaders of the Dutch Reformed Church. The school was founded to give instruction in "the learned languages and other branches of useful knowledge." Queens College opened in New Brunswick in 1771. The school made New Jersey unique. In 1776, New Jersey was the only American colony with two colleges.

Cracks in the Slave System

The Great Awakening inspired other religious groups to become interested in freedom and equality. The Quakers led the fight against slavery. In 1758, the Philadelphia Meeting of Quakers voted to pressure Quaker slave owners to free their slaves and end involvement with the slave trade.

The Lutherans held marriage ceremonies for free blacks around Hackensack, New Jersey. Some Presbyterians and Methodists accepted black Americans as equal members of their church. Between 1740 and 1782, Anglicans baptized at least 350 blacks in New Jersey. Old beliefs about the morality of slavery were beginning to crumble.

John Woolman, An American Hero

John Woolman was one of the first white Americans to speak out against the horrors of slavery. Born near Mount Holly, New Jersey, Woolman became a leader of the Quakers in Burlington in 1743. Traveling throughout the colonies, he argued for an end to slavery. In 1754, he wrote *Some Considerations on the Keeping of Negroes*. This was one of the earliest antislavery publications in America. In 1761, Woolman specifically encouraged the New Jersey Quakers to free their slaves.

The Brotherton Reservation

The Great Awakening also led to a great outburst of missionary activity intended to convert Native Americans to Christianity. During the 1740s, Moravians and Presbyterians converted some Lenni-Lenape by preaching in Native American languages and banning alcohol. Some missionaries taught reading, writing, and crafts.

In 1758, the British paid the Lenni-Lenape for their remaining land claims in New Jersey. The colony then created a 3,000-acre (1,200-hectare) reservation at Brotherton for those Lenni-Lenape wishing to remain in the state. About 200 of the "original people" moved to Brotherton. There, they made their homes in the New Jersey Pine Barrens. Most of the other Lenni-Lenape were now living in the Ohio Territory.

Unfortunately, the Brotherton Reservation did not last. Colonists in the area grazed their cattle on Lenni-Lenape land, making it unfit for planting. John Brainerd, superintendent of the reservation, wrote that the Lenni-Lenape "have observed to me that the white people lie, defraud, steal and drink worse than Indians…who before the coming of the English knew of no such thing as strong drink."

By 1801, the Lenni-Lenape of Brotherton were living in poverty. The New Jersey legislature sold the Brotherton reservation to twenty-two people for two to five dollars an acre. The few remaining Brotherton Lenni-Lenape were given $3,551. Then they moved to join other Native Americans in Oneida County, New York. In the 1800s, they moved to Wisconsin. In the year 2000, more than 10,000 people claimed some descent from the Lenni-Lenape tribe. Most lived in Oklahoma, Wisconsin, and Ontario, Canada, but several thousand still lived in New Jersey.

Moravian preachers went to Lenni-Lenape villages and tried to convert the Indians to Christianity.

Protesting the Tea Tax

In December 1773, colonists in Boston threw British tea into the harbor to protest the tax on tea. This act was called the Boston Tea Party. The British responded by closing Boston Harbor.

As a way to punish the Bostonians for their tea party, the British Parliament passed what Americans called the Intolerable Acts. They closed the port of Boston. This caused a food shortage in the city. It also resulted in the closing of many businesses. Parliament also further limited the amount of control that the people of Massachusetts had over their government.

People in all the colonies were upset by the actions of the British. Over the summer of 1774, American patriots planned a big meeting to discuss the crisis. The meeting was to be held in Philadelphia, Pennsylvania, between early September and late October of 1774. It would be called the First Continental Congress.

Most of the representatives at the First Continental Congress were not yet in favor of independence from England. But they wanted to be treated in a more respectful manner and they wanted the Intolerable Acts repealed. This Continental Congress advised Americans to boycott (refuse to buy) British goods. Essex, Bergen, Middlesex, Sussex, and

Monmouth counties, all in eastern New Jersey, quickly voiced their support for a boycott.

The First Continental Congress ended on October 26, 1774. Before the members of the Continental Congress left, they agreed that they should meet again in the spring at a Second Continental Congress.

The Provincial Congress

In April 1775, fighting broke out between the British and Americans at Lexington and Concord in Massachusetts. This was the beginning of the American Revolution.

Many colonists in New Jersey still felt loyal to Britain. Those who opposed British rule felt that they had to take action. They formed the state's first Provincial Congress. Although this congress was illegal according to British law, the group planned to meet in New Brunswick in May 1775.

The New Jersey congress did not actually support complete independence from England. In fact, it opened with a pledge of allegiance to the British king. But the representatives did vote to collect their own taxes. They organized elections. They also voted to start an army. They created their own government of New Jersey. This government would operate side by side with, but independently of, the British government.

Burnt Tea

New Jersey's most famous anti-British incident happened in Greenwich. It occurred on the night of December 22, 1774. Groups of young men dressed as Indians protested against the tea tax. They broke into a warehouse, stole a load of British tea and burned it in the village square.

The New Jersey Constitution of 1776

The first constitution of the state of New Jersey was adopted on July 2, 1776, at a Provincial Congress held at Burlington. New Jersey colonists were still not sure they wanted to separate from England. They included a section in their constitution stating that "if a reconciliation [settlement] between Great Britain and these colonies should take place…this charter shall be null and void."

The new state constitution made the governorship of New Jersey an extremely weak position. The governor could not veto (reject) laws or appoint officers. Instead, the constitution placed almost all the power in the legislature, which would even choose the governor. Voters had to have at least fifty pounds ($7,000 today) in property in order to vote. This rule allowed most male farmers and even some women and free blacks to vote.

The New Jersey constitution stated that all Protestant inhabitants would enjoy full civil rights. It did not mention members of other religions. Many settlers believed that this meant it was acceptable to **discriminate** against Jews and Catholics.

New Jersey was the only colony that allowed women to vote. Its constitution gave the vote to "all inhabitants of this colony, of full age, who are worth fifty pounds."

Independence

Colonists in New Jersey were still deeply divided about independence. But pro-independence supporters were determined to get their way. Elections were held for the New Jersey Provincial Congress in May 1776. During these elections, rebels used the threat of violence to keep Americans from voting. In some counties, frightened anti-independence men refused to run as candidates. More than half of New Jersey's eligible voters failed to vote. As a result, the new Provincial Congress supported independence.

On June 22, 1776, the Provincial Congress instructed New Jersey's representatives to the Second Continental Congress to support independence. Five New Jersey delegates signed the Declaration of Independence. They were Richard Stockton, John Hart, Francis Hopkinson, Abraham Clark, and John Witherspoon.

The important decision to fight for independence had come very quickly. Almost no one in any American colony had supported a revolution in 1774. William Livingston, New Jersey's governor from 1776 to 1790, later said that New Jersey's citizens "had themselves suffered little, if at all, from English government. Under it they had prospered and multiplied." Yet by 1776, New Jersey colonists were fighting for their lives, against the British and against each other.

William Franklin

The governor of New Jersey refused to join the pro-independence group. William Franklin was the American-born son of Benjamin Franklin, the famous scientist and politician. Young William joined his father on many trips, including those to England. He was educated in England and became a lawyer.

When he returned to America in 1763, it was as the

William Franklin

royal governor of New Jersey. The governor was well liked by the colonists of New Jersey. However, Franklin was very much against independence. In January 1775, he warned the New Jersey Assembly against destroying "that form of government of which you are an important part, and which it is your duty by all lawful means to preserve."

Although William's father, Benjamin Franklin, was a member of the Continental Congress, William Franklin worked extremely hard to prevent New Jersey from joining the independence movement. However, the royal governor had no troops to command to put down the rebels.

In June 1776, New Jersey's Provincial Congress declared Governor Franklin "an enemy of the liberties of this country." The next month, Franklin was sent to prison in Connecticut. In 1782, he was sent to England. New Jersey's last royal governor never returned to the land of his birth, but died in England in 1813.

CHAPTER SEVEN

Crossroads of the Revolution

⊛⊛⊛⊛⊛⊛⊛⊛⊛⊛⊛⊛⊛⊛⊛⊛⊛⊛⊛⊛⊛⊛⊛⊛⊛⊛⊛⊛

Patriots and Loyalists

Many New Jersey residents wanted to remain loyal to England. These **Loyalists**, also called Tories, thought of the the people who wanted independence as rioters who didn't want to pay their taxes. Almost half of the colonists in New Jersey were probably Loyalists.

The western part of New Jersey was less enthusiastic about independence than the eastern half. Quakers, who lived in the west, were often pacifists. This means that they opposed all fighting. The eastern counties provided more loans and more men to the **Patriot** cause than the west.

🐚 *Soldiers in the Continental Army were a common sight in New Jersey throughout the Revolutionary War.*

New Jersey was more divided in its loyalties than almost any other state. The results were tragic. Local residents fought each other as much as they fought the British. The Revolutionary War in New Jersey turned neighbor against neighbor.

A Strategic State

The British strategy during the Revolutionary War was to control the most important colonial cities. British troops occupied New York City in 1776 and Philadelphia in 1777. New Jersey was in a strategic position between these two cities. More than ninety battles took place there.

Patriot general George Washington and his troops crossed the state of New Jersey four times. He spent the winter with his army at Morristown twice. Once, he wintered at Middlebrook. During the Revolutionary War, Washington spent about one quarter of his time in the state of New Jersey.

In 1775, New Jersey organized a militia of Patriots who supported independence. The colony raised three battalions of regular soldiers for the Continental army.

At first, New Jersey's soldiers were enthusiastic and eager to fight for independence. But many soon grew tired of army life. They were stationed far from their homes. They were tired and missed their families.

The soliders often failed to sign up again when their one-year enlistment ended. Some did not return to the militia after going home on leave. The first two New Jersey battalions almost completely disappeared in 1776.

As they retreated from New York, General George Washington and his men looked across the Hudson River at New Jersey, where they would fight many important battles.

The Battles of Trenton and Princeton

By the fall of 1776, it seemed that the Patriots would lose the war. The British took New York City in September 1776. They drove Washington's forces out of New York, winning one battle after another. The British marched into New Jersey in November, overwhelming the state. When Washington requested the help of the New Jersey militia, not a single unit turned out. Washington wrote, "The conduct of the Jerseys has been most infamous."

British General William Howe drove Washington's army across the Delaware River into Pennsylvania by December 1776. The British occupied Trenton. Howe announced that he would forgive and protect any rebels who swore loyalty to England. Nearly 3,000 New Jersey men took up Howe's offer. They included some members of the legislature and Richard Stockton. Stockton had signed the Declaration of Independence for New Jersey less than a year earlier.

Washington managed to save his shrinking army from British troops, but now he needed a chance to counterattack. The chance came on Christmas Day. In the 1700s, armies did not usually fight during the winter. Washington, however, had other ideas. On the night of December 25, he

"Times That Try Men's Souls"

Thomas Paine was a famous author and statesman. He also served with the Continental army. He was there during Washington's gloomy retreat across New Jersey in the fall of 1776. It was in Newark that he wrote his most famous lines: "These are the times that try men's souls. The summer soldier and the sunshine patriot will, in this crisis, shrink from the service of his country; but he that stands it now, deserves the love and thanks of man and woman." This exciting challenge was read to the American troops just before the Battle of Trenton.

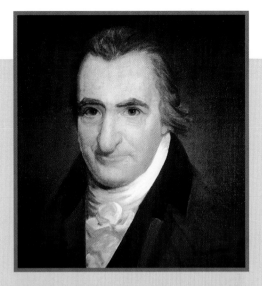

Thomas Paine's fifty-page book called Common Sense *convinced many colonists that they should declare their independence from England.*

boldly ordered his army into boats to cross the ice-filled Delaware River and attack Trenton. Washington's ragged army completely surprised the British soldiers, capturing more than 900 of them.

Washington was not yet done with his winter fighting. On January 3, 1777, the American army attacked the British at Princeton. The Americans won another victory. In two weeks, Washington had completely changed the course of the war. The British army abandoned most of New Jersey, concentrating its forces between Perth Amboy and New Brunswick. More importantly, Washington's two victories boosted sagging American spirits and restored the confidence of the Patriots.

The Battle of Monmouth

Although the Patriots defeated the British at Trenton and Princeton, the war was not over. In 1777, the American army crushed the British at Saratoga, New York. But the British defeated Washington in Pennsylvania, at Germantown and Brandywine Creek. While the British wintered in comfortable Philadelphia, the Americans shivered at Valley Forge in Pennsylvania. The soldiers were starving and half-frozen.

Molly Pitcher

The Battle of Monmouth lasted all day, with the temperature reaching nearly 100 degrees Fahrenheit (38 degrees Celsius). Men and horses collapsed from heat stroke and exhaustion. Legend tells of "Molly Pitcher," Mary Ludwig Hays (later McCauley), at the battle. She earned her nickname by carrying heavy buckets of water to the Patriots, who were firing cannons in the brutal heat. When her soldier husband was overcome with heat exhaustion, Molly took his place. She helped the soldiers fire the cannons.

But the American army did not fall apart. In fact, Baron von Steuben, a German volunteer serving in the American army, used the time to turn Washington's inexperienced soldiers into an organized and powerful army.

In June 1778, Washington's "new" Continental army faced its first test. British general Henry Clinton decided to abandon Philadelphia. He wanted to move his army back to New York City. On June 28, Washington chose Monmouth Courthouse (now Freehold) as the place to intercept the British.

The Patriots were almost crushed when General Charles Lee disobeyed George Washington's orders and ordered a retreat. Washington, von Steuben, and General Nathanael Greene arrived just in time to prevent a disaster. The Americans fought bravely. One New Jersey officer proudly wrote that the Americans had "engaged the flower of the British army" and beaten "the proud King's-Guards and haughty British-Grenadiers & gained Immortal-honor."

Neighbor Against Neighbor

In New Jersey, Loyalists and Patriots took turns burning and looting their neighbors' houses. It was not unusual for brothers to be divided against brothers. Nor was it unusual for fathers to be against sons, like Benjamin and William Franklin.

Throughout New Jersey, Loyalists and their Patriot neighbors fought a savage war. In Monmouth, David Forman's Patriot "Retaliators" burned the homes of anyone they didn't like. In the Long Beach Island Massacre, Loyalist John Bacon murdered twenty-one militiamen while they slept on a beach in 1782. In the Hackensack Valley community of Schraalenburgh, Patriots looted farms and homesteads throughout the countryside. One of the most horrible incidents took place at the Hancock House in Salem in 1778. A British force of nearly 300 men under John Simcoe surprised and massacred a small band of sleeping colonial militiamen.

William Livingston became New Jersey's governor in 1776. In March 1777, he created a twelve-man Council of Safety. The council tried to force all suspected supporters of England in New Jersey to pledge allegiance to the Patriots.

The Death of Hannah Caldwell

Civilians who stayed in New Jersey ran risks. Hannah Caldwell was the wife of James Caldwell, a well-known Patriot. She was shot through the window of a house at the Battle of Connecticut Farms, New Jersey, in 1780. Although she was probably killed by a stray bullet, Patriots insisted she had been intentionally shot by a Loyalist, while holding a baby in her arms. The story of her death angered New Jersey Patriots and made them more determined than ever to defeat the British.

Livingston's council tried hundreds of suspected Loyalists for treason. Many were hanged. Livingston's extreme tactics helped swing New Jersey to the Patriot cause.

Some civilians (people not serving in the army) fled New Jersey. Many Loyalists moved to British-occupied New York. Some suspected Loyalists were exiled. Women were expected to always take the same sides as their husbands.

Mary Ludwig Hays, known as Molly Pitcher, brought water to the American troops during the battle of Monmouth and fought in her husband's place when he was overcome by the heat.

In 1777, the New Jersey legislature passed a law "to send into the Enemy's Line such of the wives and Children of Persons lately residing within this State, who have gone over to the Enemy."

A Troubled Army

Washington and his army camped for the winter of 1779–1780 outside Morristown. The winter was one of the coldest on record. The snowdrifts were 12 feet (3.6 meters) high, and travel was impossible. The Continental army could not get food. Washington wrote that his half-starved soldiers took shelter in cold log huts and ate "every kind of horse food but hay." Tempe Wick, a young girl who lived

nearby, supposedly hid her horse in her bedroom because she was afraid the soldiers would eat it.

American soldiers often went unpaid for months at a time. From 1779 to 1781, several groups of soldiers stationed in New Jersey protested their lack of pay by staging a mutiny (refusing to follow orders). New Jersey's own soldiers mutinied several times.

Military Hospitals

In the 1700s, few people understood that germs can lead to infection and illness. Soldiers' wounds often became infected by unclean conditions or poor medical care. Soldiers died just as frequently in military hospitals as when they were left with their friends or families. The few hospitals that existed did not have enough nurses. A doctor at a hospital in Perth Amboy noted that "there are so few women and so many men to work for...the sick must suffer much unless well nursed and kept clean."

Many New Jersey residents on both sides took advantage of the soldiers. They knew that the soldiers had little money. Merchants sold food and supplies at very high prices to the already struggling men. A New Jersey law of 1777 fined anyone who had blankets to sell and intentionally sold them at an "exorbitant price."

Some people did make sacrifices for the Patriot cause. In July 1780, New Jersey Patriot women advertised that they would raise money "for the relief and encouragement of those brave Men...who...so repeatedly suffered, fought, and bled in the cause of virtue and their oppressed country." Patriot women from thirteen New Jersey counties raised more than $15,000. However, the price of almost everything had gone up because of the war. The money bought only 380 pairs of socks for New Jersey soldiers.

Fighting With Words

Patience Lovell Wright from Bordentown was a famous painter and wax sculptor during the Revolutionary War years. While working in England, she may have acted as an American spy during the war. Wright supposedly sent secret messages to the Patriots about British troop movements. The messages were hidden in wax sculptures.

Philip Freneau supported the war with his pen, as well as his gun. Freneau wrote many poems supporting the Patriot cause. He was known as "the Poet of the Revolution." In 1781, he wrote a long poem called "The British Prison Ship." It told the story of his capture by the British. Many people consider Freneau the earliest important American poet.

Black Americans and the Revolution

The Declaration of Independence stated that every person had natural rights, but it did not mention the topic of slavery. The British offered freedom to slaves who joined their side. Most black Americans, therefore, chose to support the king of England. Hundreds of runaway slaves fled New Jersey for British-occupied New York City. Many ex-slaves served in the British army. After the war, they escaped to Canada.

The original Declaration of Independence was handwritten by Thomas Jefferson.

In New Jersey, most Patriots supported slavery. Patriot governor William Livingston did not. He wrote that slavery was "utterly inconsistent with the principles of Christianity & humanity & in America, who have almost idolized liberty, particularly…disgraceful." Another brave Patriot was Jacob Green, a Presbyterian minister in Hanover. In 1778, he delivered a sermon: "Can it be believed that a people contending for liberty should at the same time be supporting slavery?… I cannot but think that our practicing Negro Slavery is the most crying sin in our land." As a result, a New Jersey mob destroyed his church.

The War Ends

By the end of the war, about 4,000 New Jersey men had served in the Continental army. Another 10,000 saw some other kind of military duty, usually with the militia. Much of the state was in ruins, especially in the east. Joseph Reed was Washington's aide and a native of New Jersey. He told his wife, "It is of little consequence which army passes. It is equally destructive to friend and foe."

Many of New Jersey's Loyalists never returned to the state. In 1777, the New Jersey legislature claimed and sold the properties of hundreds of Loyalists. When the war ended, some tried to return but found they were not welcome. A **petition** from Monmouth County asked the state legislature not to let Loyalists return. It called them "bloodthirsty robbers" and "atrocious monsters." Thousands of former New Jersey residents left the country and moved to Nova Scotia, Canada.

In 1781, the Patriots won an important victory over the British at Yorktown, Virginia. The British decided that the war was too costly and surrendered. In the Treaty of Paris of 1783, England accepted that America was independent. New Jersey was no longer a colony of England. The people of New Jersey rejoiced that peace had come again.

CHAPTER EIGHT

A New State in a New Nation

A "Small" State

On November 25, 1783, thousands of New Jersey residents stood on the heights of Bergen and the shores of Elizabeth to watch an amazing sight. Across the water, a British fleet of more than 400 ships was departing from New York City. The ships were taking the British army back to England.

New Jersey's population had increased from about 15,000 in 1700 to more than 180,000 by 1783. New Jersey was still one of the small states, both in size and in population. Yet New Jersey had an important place in the new nation.

Crowds along the Hudson River in New York and New Jersey cheered as the last boatload of British soldiers left New York in 1783.

New Jersey had suffered a great deal in the Revolutionary War. The British occupation and the brutal fighting between Patriots and Loyalists had destroyed the state. The New Jersey legislature printed more paper money to help rebuild the state. However, this only led to **inflation**. New Jersey's money became so worthless that merchants in New York City and Philadelphia refused to accept it. In addition, New York and New Jersey were arguing over the right to tax products being sold in their states. The new government of the United States of America would have to address these problems.

The New Jersey Plan

America needed to be reorganized now that it was an independent nation and not a group of British colonies. At the time, the American government was based on a document called the Articles of Confederation. Some people thought that this government was too weak. Representatives from the states met at the Constitutional Convention in Philadelphia in the summer of 1787. They wanted to create a stronger national government. New Jersey sent five representatives: David Brearly, William Houston, William Paterson, William Livingston, and Jonathan Dayton.

James Madison favored a strong national government for the new United States and wanted the population of each state to determine the number of votes it had in Congress.

James Madison of Virginia believed that a completely new constitution had to be written for the country. He arrived in Philadelphia with a plan, known as the Virginia Plan, which would create a very strong national government. Madison's government would be based on the population of each state. At the time, Virginia's population was twice as large as New York's. It was four times larger than New Jersey's, and more than ten times the size of Delaware's population. Madison's plan would have greatly favored Virginia.

At the Constitutional Convention, New Jersey spoke for the smaller states. On June 15, 1787, Paterson, the former attorney general of New Jersey, offered his own proposal, known as the New Jersey Plan. Paterson suggested keeping the basic system of the Articles of Confederation. The articles created only one lawmaking group. Within this group, each state had one vote. Paterson thought this was fair. Why should New Jersey join the United States if Virginia could outvote it every time?

The argument over representation lasted for a month. On July 16, the Constitutional Convention settled on a compromise. It created a House of Representatives chosen directly by the people. It also formed another governing body called the Senate. Members of the Senate would be chosen by state legislatures. In the House of Representatives, each state would be represented according to its population. But each state would have two votes in the Senate, no matter what its size.

The Constitution Can Be Changed

The framers of the Constitution originally gave the state legislatures the power to choose the senators. Today, however, members of the U.S. Senate are elected directly by the people. The change was made in the Seventeenth Amendment in 1913 in order to make the Senate more democratic.

To make a law, both the Senate and the House of Representatives would have to approve. This compromise was closer to Paterson's New Jersey Plan than to Madison's Virginia Plan. The compromise was a great victory for the states that were less populated.

Printed copies of the Constitution were sent to each state so that voters could read it.

Approval

The American states now had to **ratify** (or approve) the new Constitution. In many states, opponents of the Constitution tried to prevent its ratification. However, there was almost no opposition to the new Constitution in New Jersey. Elias Boudinot, one of New Jersey's leading Patriots, worked very hard to ensure the state's approval.

William Livingston was governor of New Jersey from 1776 until his death in 1790.

On December 18, 1787, after only three days of debate, New Jersey ratified the new Constitution. The vote was thirty-eight to zero. With this action, New Jersey officially became the third state of the United States.

In the summer of 1790, long-time governor William Livingston died. The New Jersey legislature appointed William Paterson to succeed him. Paterson would be the state's first governor under the Constitution. New Jersey gave up the twin capitals at Burlington and Perth Amboy. Trenton was chosen as the state capital in 1790. At the time, it consisted of little more than a few muddy public streets. However, the city was almost halfway between New York City and Philadelphia. It became an important stopover on the trade route between these cities.

Slavery

The Constitution not only allowed slavery but also protected it. However, discussions of "freedom" during the Revolutionary War had some effect. By 1787, most northern states had begun the process that would end slavery in the north.

According to the first U.S. census of 1790, there were still more than 30,000 slaves in the north. New Jersey had 11,423 slaves. Slaves made up about 6 percent of New Jersey's population of 170,000. Slavery remained common in many rural areas. In Bergen County, whites held more than 2,000 black Americans in slavery. There were also more than 1,000 slaves in each of the counties of Essex, Hunterdon, Middlesex, Monmouth, and Somerset. Slavery was actually increasing in western New Jersey townships such as Franklin and Harrington.

At the same time, about 3,000 free blacks lived in New Jersey. They made up less than 2 percent of the state's population. The largest number of free blacks lived in Burlington County. Some blacks tried to escape white prejudice by forming their own communities in New Jersey. For example, the small community of Skunk Hollow in Bergen County was home to more than twenty black families. Many of them were former slaves.

The Beginning of the End of Slavery

Black Americans, both enslaved and free, had always struggled to end slavery. Some white New Jersey residents now joined this struggle. They supported the **abolition** (ending) of slavery in the state. In 1786, Governor William Livingston pressured the New Jersey legislature to change the law. Bringing new slaves into the state from Africa or the West Indies was now prohibited.

New Jersey was the last northern state to pass laws against slavery. In 1804, the legislature approved a gradual

Groups of New Jersey's freed slaves took their belongings and moved into small communities such as Skunk Hollow and Dunkerhook.

emancipation act. (Emancipation was the freeing of slaves.) The law did not free the slaves immediately. Instead, it said that any slaves born after 1804 would be free after serving the masters of their mothers for a certain time. They had to serve until they were twenty-eight (males) or twenty-five (females). This meant there would still be slaves in New Jersey for many years. The U.S. census of 1830 reported that only 3,568 black Americans remained slaves in the northern United States. More than two-thirds of these resided in New Jersey.

The Right to Vote

The Declaration of Independence stated that the people should elect the government. But not everyone agreed on who the people were. Black Americans and women made up more than half the population of New Jersey. In 1790, the New Jersey legislature passed an election law. The law referred to the state's voters as "he" and "she." This seemed to mean that both men and women had the right to vote in New Jersey. In 1797, the legislature passed another election law. This law specifically stated that "all free inhabitants of this State, of full age, who are worth fifty pounds" could vote. The law again referred to New Jersey's voters as "he" and "she."

"All Men Are Created Equal"

Some New Jersey residents took the Declaration of Independence very seriously. On July 4, 1783, slave owner Moses Bloomfield mounted a platform in Woodbridge. He was joined by his fourteen slaves. Bloomfield spoke to the crowd. "As a nation, we are free and independent—all men are created equal, and why should these, my fellow-citizens—my equals, be held in bondage? From this day forth they are emancipated and I hereby declare them free and absolved from all servitude to men and my posterity."

"All free inhabitants" meant that free blacks could also vote. Women and free blacks did vote in New Jersey elections in the 1790s and early 1800s. New Jersey was one of the only states to allow such democracy.

However, in 1807, New Jersey amended its state constitution to read that voters had to be "free, white male citizens of this state, of the age of twenty-one years, worth fifty pounds." By this act, women and free blacks lost their right to vote. Women would not regain the vote for more than 100 years.

A New Nation

New Jersey and the other twelve states had done what no one had believed was possible. They had broken free from a powerful country and formed a new nation. The thirteen colonies would grow to fifty and the United States of America would truly become a place where all people of all nationalities and all religions could live side by side.

Recipe
Pepper Pot Soup

During the cold winters experienced by the colonists they often ate soups like this one. An old legend says that George Washington created the original Pepper Pot soup. The soup was a huge success because it required few ingredients. Tripe was the only meat available at the time.

Sausage has been substituted for tripe in the version below.

1 tablespoon butter
1/3 cup finely diced onions
1/2 cup celery cut into small pieces
1/4 cup diced ham
6 cups water
3 chicken bouillon cubes
3 beef bouillon cubes
1/2 cup green pepper diced
1 16 oz. can diced tomatoes in juice
3/4 pound cooked sausage
1 cup cooked wild or other rice

- Melt butter in a large pot.
- Add onions, celery, green pepper, and ham. Sauté and stir mixture until vegetables are tender.
- Add water and bouillon cubes.
- Cook until bouillon cubes dissolve in mixture.
- Add remaining ingredients. Simmer for 20 minutes and serve.

This activity should be done with adult supervision.

Activity

Rag Doll

Colonial parents and children often created their own toys. These toys were made from whatever was around the house. An example is the rag doll that was usually crafted from found materials like old cloth or even corncobs.

Directions

Newspaper or butcher paper for pattern • Fabric or old towels or sheets • Stuffing (cotton, newspaper, rags, fabric scraps) Pins • Needle • Thread • Scissors Yarn • Buttons • Markers

• Make a pattern by drawing the doll's outline on a sheet of newspaper in the desired size. Cut out the doll pattern.

• Place and pin the doll pattern on two layers of fabric, towel, or sheet. Using a pencil or marker, trace the pattern. Leave room to allow for two-inch seams. Cut out the doll. Remove the pattern.

• Place the two cut-out doll patterns on top of each other.

If your fabric has a pattern, place the two "good" sides facing each other.

• Sew the pieces together, leaving a two-inch border all around the doll. Leave an opening of about two inches. Turn the doll inside out.

• Stuff the cotton, rags, or newspaper pieces through the opening inside the doll. Sew the opening closed when the doll is fully stuffed.

• Glue yarn hair on the doll's head. Let dry. Glue on two button eyes and a small piece of red cloth for the mouth. If red cloth is unavailable, use red paint or a marker to make the mouth. Use a marker to create a nose.

This activity should be done with adult supervision.

NEW JERSEY
Time Line

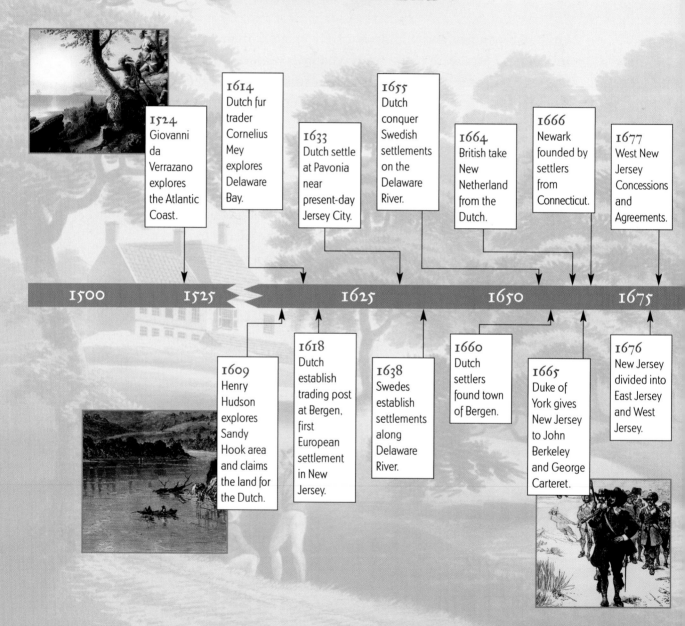

1524 Giovanni da Verrazano explores the Atlantic Coast.

1614 Dutch fur trader Cornelius Mey explores Delaware Bay.

1633 Dutch settle at Pavonia near present-day Jersey City.

1655 Dutch conquer Swedish settlements on the Delaware River.

1664 British take New Netherland from the Dutch.

1666 Newark founded by settlers from Connecticut.

1677 West New Jersey Concessions and Agreements.

1500   1525   1625   1650   1675

1609 Henry Hudson explores Sandy Hook area and claims the land for the Dutch.

1618 Dutch establish trading post at Bergen, first European settlement in New Jersey.

1638 Swedes establish settlements along Delaware River.

1660 Dutch settlers found town of Bergen.

1665 Duke of York gives New Jersey to John Berkeley and George Carteret.

1676 New Jersey divided into East Jersey and West Jersey.

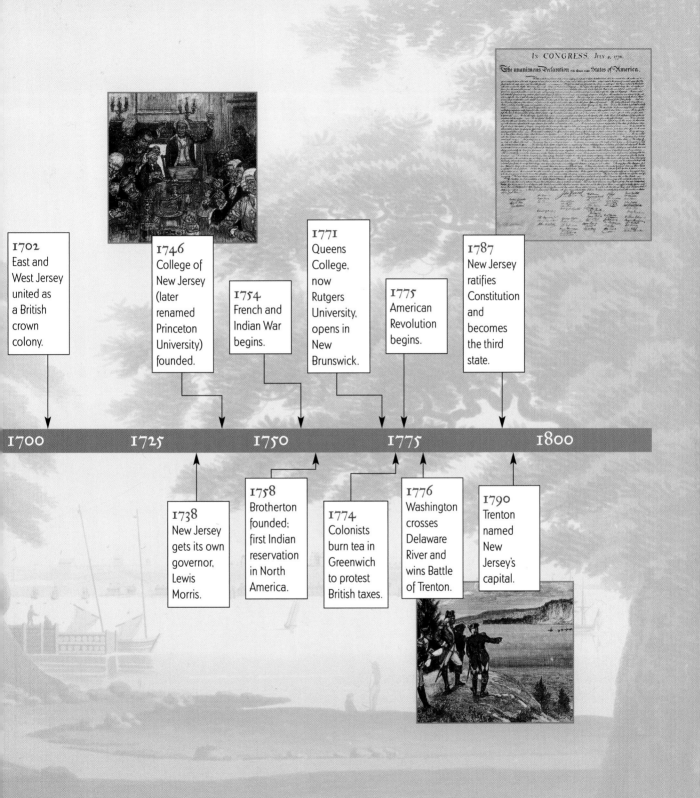

1702
East and West Jersey united as a British crown colony.

1746
College of New Jersey (later renamed Princeton University) founded.

1754
French and Indian War begins.

1771
Queens College, now Rutgers University, opens in New Brunswick.

1775
American Revolution begins.

1787
New Jersey ratifies Constitution and becomes the third state.

1700   **1725**   **1750**   **1775**   **1800**

1738
New Jersey gets its own governor, Lewis Morris.

1758
Brotherton founded; first Indian reservation in North America.

1774
Colonists burn tea in Greenwich to protest British taxes.

1776
Washington crosses Delaware River and wins Battle of Trenton.

1790
Trenton named New Jersey's capital.

Further Reading

Aylesworth, Thomas, and Virginia Aylesworth. *Upper Atlantic: New Jersey, New York.* New York, NY: Chelsea House, 1996.

Fleming, Thomas. *New Jersey; A History.* New York, NY: W. W. Norton, 1977.

Grumet, Robert. *The Lenapes.* New York, NY: Chelsea House, 1989.

Hodges, Graham. *Root and Branch: African Americans in New York and East Jersey, 1613-1863.* Chapel Hill, NC: University of North Carolina Press, 1999.

Moragne, Wendy. *Celebrate the States: New Jersey.* New York, NY: Benchmark, 2000.

Tunis, Edwin. *Colonial Living.* New York, NY: Thomas Crowell, 1957.

Glossary

abolition the ending of slavery in the United States

census an official count of all the people living in a place

clan a group of families claiming a common ancestor

cradle scythe a tool that catches stalks of grain as they are cut so that they can be laid flat

discriminate to be prejudiced against people and treat them unfairly

inflation a general increase in prices

Jersey wagon a large cart or carriage used in colonial New Jersey

Loyalist someone who remained loyal to the British cause in the American Revolution

mahogany a dark red-brown wood from a tropical tree used for making furniture

marl a loose soil mixture, often containing clay and shells, that is used as fertilizer

militia volunteer citizen-soldiers as opposed to professional soldiers

Parliament the national legislature of Great Britain

Patriot someone who sided with the colonists fighting the British in the American Revolution

patroon Dutch landholder in New York or New Jersey who was granted land and certain rights in exchange for bringing fifty new settlers to the colony

petition a letter signed by many people asking those in power to change their policies or actions

privateer privately owned ship licensed by a government to attack another country's merchant ships and steal their cargo

quitrent a token payment paid forever to the original owner of a piece of land

ratify to approve or accept by a formal agreement

redware a type of naturally-colored colonial clay pottery

repeal to revoke or take back

self-sufficient able to do things without help, especially referring to farmers

sickle a curved metal blade used in farming

Index